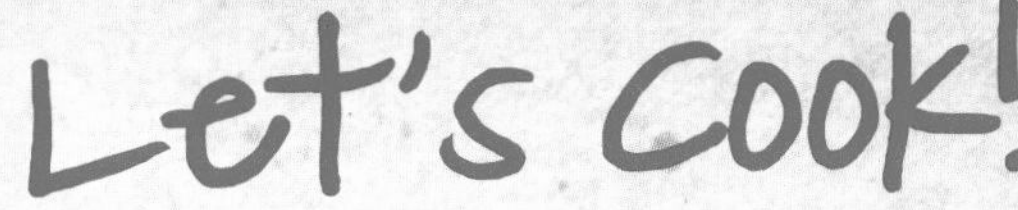

France

The Culture and Recipes of France

Tracey Kelly

PowerKiDS press

Published in 2017 by
The Rosen Publishing Group, Inc.
29 East 21st Street, New York, NY 10010

Cataloging-in-Publication Data
Names: Kelly, Tracey.
Title: Culture and recipes of France / Tracey Kelly.
Description: New York : PowerKids Press, 2017. | Series: Let's cook! | Includes index.
Identifiers: ISBN 9781508153450 (pbk.) | ISBN 9781499432572 (library bound) | ISBN 9781499431773 (6 pack)
Subjects: LCSH: Cooking, French--Juvenile literature. | Food habits--France--Juvenile literature.
Classification: LCC TX719.K455 2017 | DDC 641.5944--dc23

For Brown Bear Books Ltd:
Text and Editor: Tracey Kelly
Editorial Director: Lindsey Lowe
Children's Publisher: Anne O'Daly
Design Manager: Keith Davis
Designer: Melissa Roskell
Picture Manager: Sophie Mortimer

Picture Credits: t=top, c=center, b=bottom, l=left, r=right. Front Cover: Shutterstock: WDG Photo c, Brent Hofacker r, Alxcrs r, neftali r, Mirka Markova l, LanaN l, milezaway t. Inside: 1, Dreamstime: 33b, Peter Lovas 39; Shutterstock: 5, 8-9t, 9b, 10bl, 15b, 30-31t, 35b, 36-37b, 41b, Felix Catana 28-29t, Elenor Dijour 38t, Pierre Jean Durieu 22-23, Geoffrey Gerber 8-9b, Jari Hindstroem 38b, Victor Kiev 21l, Veniamin Kraskov 10-11t, Alexander Leonov 31b, Timofeyeva Lyubov 27bl, Margouilat Photo 25br, 45b, Mirka Markova 1l, Monkey Business Images 28-29b, Tanguy Mouahidine 7b, neftali 1bl, Roman Prishenko 23br, Radu Razvan 22, Sea Wave 17b, Elana Shahkina 30, Boris, Strougjko 6-7t, Tatyana Tomsickova 6bl, Julie Vader 20, Jouau Viatchaslau 20-21b, Didier Wuthrich 4l; Thinkstock: istockphoto 43b, Anne Mastenbroek 11br, Monkey Business Images 36-37t.

Special thanks to Klaus Arras for all other photography.

Manufactured in the United States of America
CPSIA Compliance Information: Batch #BW17PK: For Further Information contact Rosen Publishing, New York, New York at 1-800-237-9932.

Contents

Looking at France

France is the largest country in western Europe and one of the oldest nations on Earth. From its beautiful countryside to its vibrant cities, France is rich in history and culture. And it is famous for its delicious food!

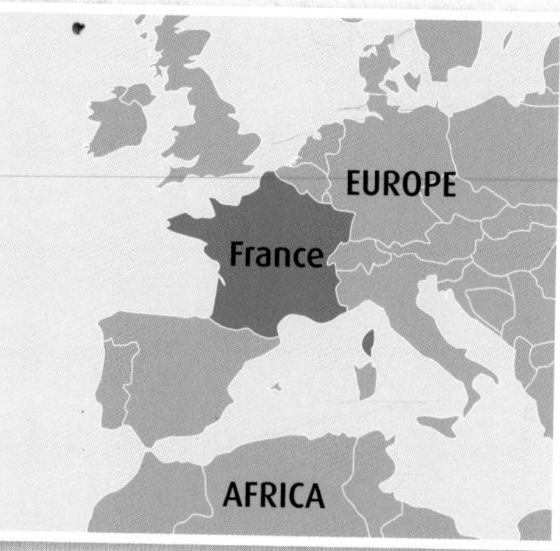

France is bordered by the European countries of Spain, Belgium, Luxembourg, Germany, Switzerland, and Italy.

Vive la France!

People from all over the world live in France and feed into its dynamic culture. As well as its cuisine, France is famous for art, music, fashion, architecture, sports, and literature. Around 80 million tourists visit each year, soaking up the chic fashion, great food, and amazing art. At the Louvre Museum in Paris, 9 million visitors per year view artist Leonardo da Vinci's *Mona Lisa*. But it´s not just the cities that attract visitors. France´s landscape offers up a breathtaking range of scenery, from sunny beaches and harbors, to stunning mountains and gentle plains farther inland. Vive la France (Long Live France)!

The crunchy baguette is the most common type of bread eaten by the French.

Mont St.-Michel is a rocky island off the Normandy coast. This ancient monastery gives it its name.

Paris is the capital of France. It lies on the Seine River in northern France. The Eiffel Tower is one of the city's famous landmarks.

NETHERLANDS
BELGIUM
Lille
ARDENNES
Seine
Mont St.-Michel
NORMANDY
BRITTANY
Paris
Strasbourg
Orléans
Loire
Loire
FRANCE
ATLANTIC OCEAN
Lyon
AUVERGNE
Bordeaux
Garonne
Rhône
PROVENCE
AQUITAINE
Toulouse
Marseilles
PYRENEEES
SPAIN
MEDITERRANEAN SEA

Provence is a region in southeastern France. It is famous for its bright purple lavender fields. Lavender has a strong fragrance and is used in perfumes and soaps.

The Northwest

The long, windswept coastlines of Normandy and Brittany are dotted with sandy beaches and rugged cliffs. Inland, ancient villages date from medieval days. The Catholic saint Joan of Arc was burned at the stake in Rouen in 1431. William the Conqueror, who conquered England in 1066, is buried in Caen. Brittany's medieval ports, such as Brest and St. Nazaire, are known for fishing, shipbuilding, and sea trading. The port of St. Malo was once notorious for pirates!

This is the Fort La Latte, a castle on the Côte de Granit Rose (Pink Granite Coast) in Brittany.

Château de Chambord is a massive castle in the Loire Valley. It has 440 rooms and 13 staircases.

Central France

The Auvergne region is an area of great natural beauty. Cyclists, nature lovers, and hikers flock to its regional parks, and relax in its spring-fed spas, such as Vichy. In the east, the snowy French Alps mountain range attracts thousands of skiers during winter. Burgundy is a famous wine-growing region that stretches down to the city of Lyons, which the French consider to be the food capital of France. Also known for its vineyards, the lush Loire Valley is home to thousands of magnificent châteaux, or castles.

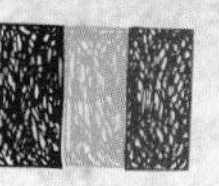

Southern France

The Pyrenees Mountains separate France from Spain and Portugal. They stretch for 270 miles (434 kilometers). The varied landscape ranges from dense forest to granite cliffs and snow-capped peaks. People visit the Pyrenees National Park to hike, mountain climb, and see wild animals, such as brown bears and mountain goats.

Sun-drenched Provence is a region that delights tourists, with its breathtaking scenery and Mediterranean coastline. During summer vacation, Europeans head for the Cote d'Azur (in English, called the French Riviera) to relax and meet family and friends. For decades, glamorous towns such as Nice, Cannes, and St.Tropez have been fashionable places to swim, sunbathe—and be seen!

DID YOU KNOW?

A château is a castle or large house, and France has about 40,000 of them! Some are enormous and vast, but others look just like simple farmhouses. Any building on a vineyard estate can call itself a château—whether it has castle turrets or not!

A clear, blue lake is surrounded by enormous mountains in the Pyrenees National Park.

Food and Farming

France has one of the most important farming industries in western Europe. Each region has a wonderful variety of speciality foods.

Northern Menu

France is well known for dairy products. In Normandy, brown and white Normande cows produce the milk that goes into the region's world-famous cheeses. These include Camembert, Livarot, and Comté. The town of Isigny produces rich cream and butter, ingredients used in many local dishes.

Bread is eaten at most meals, so cereal crops are important. In Brittany, wheat and buckwheat are grown. Their flours are used to make crêpes and gallettes (a savory buckwheat crêpe) as well. Brioche, a small, light, sweet roll, is another bakery specialty.

The French are passionate about cheese, or *fromage*. From creamy varieties, such as Brie and Camembert, to hard cheeses like Cantal and Comté, they feature at many meals.

Cows graze in a field in Normandy. Their milk is used to make the region's famous dairy foods.

Central Gardens

The Loire Valley is sometimes called the "Garden of France," because fruit and vegetables grow well in its rich soil. Pears and apples are grown in Anjou and Touraine. Vineyards in the Loire—and in the nearby regions of Rhône and Burgundy—produce some of the finest wines in the world. Almost half of the mushrooms eaten in France are grown in limestone caves along the Loire River.

Charcuterie (cold cooked meats and sausages) are important to the French diet. Many of these are made from animals that graze in the Dauphiné Alps and Savoyard. *Charcuterie* is made from traditional pork and also from wild boar, chicken, and goose. Chicken reared in the town of Bresse (*poulet de Bresse*) is said to be the tastiest in the world!

DID YOU KNOW?

More than 400 delicious types of cheese are made in France. That is more than enough for a different cheese every day of the year!

Most towns and villages in the countryside have a weekly market. This stand is selling fresh, local fruits.

Southern Fare

The Aquitaine region is famous for its poultry-based cuisine. Ducks and geese are bred to make pâté, duck breast, and goose gizzards. Duck and goose fat are used to add flavor to many dishes. The area is also known for its dairy farms and fruit orchards.

Walnut trees and sunflower crops are grown in Perigord and Quercy. The walnuts and sunflowers are used to make cooking oils.

Garlic is an important ingredient in French cuisine, and the Languedoc region grows some of the most flavorful. Languedoc is also known for its fine wines and delicious pitted fruits, such as peaches and apricots.

Sunflowers are grown in southwestern France. The seeds are eaten or used to make oil.

Mediterranean Diet

The Mediterranean diet is one of the healthiest in the world. People who eat from its fresh, colorful vegetables, fish, pasta, and olive oil are said to live longer than those with meat-heavy diets. In Provence, farmers grow garlic, peppers, tomatoes, eggplants, olives, and fennel. Provence also has the perfect climate for growing herbs and scented lavender, used in cooking, cosmetics, and soaps.

Large, juicy beef tomatoes and purple garlic tempt passersby in markets everywhere in Provence.

Coastal Catch

With hundreds of miles of coastline and five major rivers, it's not surprising that France has some of the best fish and seafood in Europe. Normandy is known for its huge catches of oysters and scallops. In Brittany, fresh crabs are caught near St. Malo, and Cameret is known for its lobsters. On the coast west of Bordeaux, all kinds of shellfish are caught. Freshwater fish, such as perch, salmon, and pike, are fished in the rivers of the Loire Valley. They are served fresh in local cuisine.

Honfleur is a picturesque fishing village on the French Normandy coast. Fishing boats unload their daily catch at its quayside.

Let's Start Cooking

One thing's for sure—cooking is a lot of fun! In this book, you will learn about different ingredients, which tastes go together, and new cooking methods. Some recipes have steps that you'll need help with, so you can ask a parent or another adult. When your delicious meal is ready, you can serve it to family and friends.

This line tells you how many people the meal will feed.

Serves 4–6

In this box, you find out which ingredients you need for your meal.

Before you begin, check that you have everything you need. Get all the ingredients ready before you start cooking.

YOU WILL NEED

- 5 ounces milk chocolate or semisweet chocolate (or half of each)
- 2 large eggs
- 2 tablespoons confectioner's sugar

WARNING!

When to Get Help

Most cooking involves chopping ingredients and heating them in some way, whether it's frying, boiling, or baking. Be careful as you cook—and make sure your adult kitchen assistant is around to help!

TOP TIP

You can choose any chocolate you like.

Top Tip gives you more information about the recipe or the ingredients.

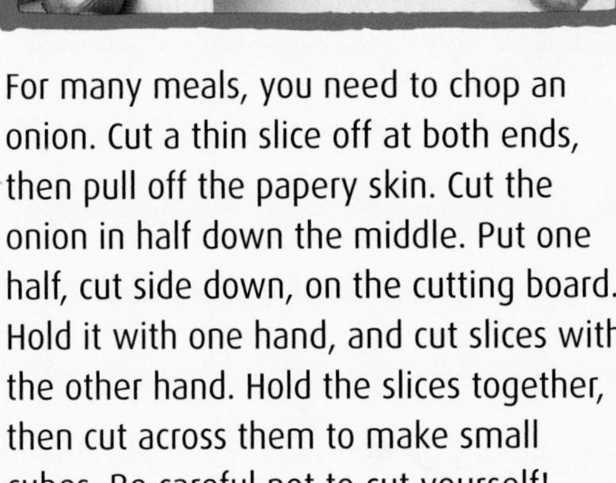

For many meals, you need to chop an onion. Cut a thin slice off at both ends, then pull off the papery skin. Cut the onion in half down the middle. Put one half, cut side down, on the cutting board. Hold it with one hand, and cut slices with the other hand. Hold the slices together, then cut across them to make small cubes. Be careful not to cut yourself!

Some recipes in this book use fresh garlic. Take a whole head of garlic, and break it into separate cloves. Cut the top and the bottom off each clove, and pull off the papery skin. You can chop the garlic clove with a sharp knife, or use a garlic press to crush the garlic directly into the skillet or saucepan.

METRIC CONVERSIONS

Oven Temperature

°F	°C
275	140
300	150
325	170
350	180
375	190
400	200
425	220
450	230
475	240

Liquid

Cups	Milliliters
¼	60
½	120
¾	180
1	240

Weight

Ounces	Grams
1	30
2	60
3	85
4	115
5	140
6	175
7	200
8	225

Sugar

Cups	Grams
¼	50
½	100
¾	150
1	200

Flour

Cups	Grams
¼	30
½	60
¾	90
1	120

Alsace Onion Tart

Serves 6

This savory tart comes from the Alsace region in eastern France. You can eat it hot or cold, but it tastes great served hot with a salad.

YOU WILL NEED

FOR THE DOUGH:
- 2 cups all-purpose flour
- 1/2 teaspoon salt
- 1 egg
- 1 2/3 cups chilled butter

FOR THE TOPPING:
- 1 pound 5 ounces onions
- 1 stick butter
- salt, black pepper
- 1/2 teaspoon paprika
- 2 tablespoons flour
- 1 cup milk
- 2 egg yolks
- 1 cup heavy cream
- 4 ounces lean smoked ham
- 4 ounces Gruyère cheese

PLUS:
- 1 quiche dish, 11 inches (28 cm) wide

1 Mix all the dough ingredients together. Knead, and shape into a ball. Wrap the dough in plastic wrap, then chill for 1 hour. Meanwhile, peel the onions, then cut them into very thin slices (see page 13). Separate the slices into rings.

2 Melt half the butter in a skillet. Add the onion rings and fry. Stir for 3 minutes, until they are golden. Season with salt, pepper, and paprika.

3 Put the rest of the butter in another skillet, and melt it. Add the flour, stir, and fry until it's golden. Add milk, a little at a time, and keep stirring. Cook over low heat for about 5 minutes, then take the skillet off the heat. Stir in the egg yolks and cream. Finally, add the onions.

5 Spread the onion mixture onto the dough. Chop the ham into cubes, and grate the cheese. Sprinkle them over the tart. Bake for 40 minutes. Leave it for 10 minutes before cutting.

4 Preheat the oven to 400°F. Knead the dough again, then roll it out thinly. Line the quiche dish with the dough. Cut off any dough that sticks over the top of the dish.

TOP TIP

Instead of making the dough yourself, you could use store-bought pastry. Choose puff pastry for a lighter crust.

Potato Gratin

Serves 3-4

Gratin dauphinois (say "gra-tan doh-fee-nwa") is from Grenoble. Bake these tasty scalloped potatoes until they're golden and crunchy.

YOU WILL NEED

- 1 pound waxy potatoes, for example, Yukon Gold
- 2 garlic cloves
- 2 tablespoons butter (plus some more to grease the aluminum foil)
- 3 eggs
- $1\frac{2}{3}$ cups heavy cream or milk
- salt, white pepper
- parsley, to garnish

1 Preheat the oven to 400°F. Wash and peel the potatoes. Cut them into thin slices.

TOP TIP

Use potatoes that are about the same size, so that they take about the same time to cook.

2 Peel and chop the garlic. Melt the butter in a skillet until it foams. Fry the garlic in the butter. Add the garlic and butter to a gratin dish. Spread them around to grease the dish.

3 Put the potato slices in the dish in overlapping circles.

4 In a bowl, whisk the eggs with the cream or milk. Season with salt and black pepper, then pour it over the potatoes.

5 Grease a sheet of aluminum foil with butter. Put the foil over the dish. Bake in the oven for about 20 minutes.

6 Remove the foil, and continue baking for another 30 to 40 minutes, until the potatoes start to look golden brown. Check that the potatoes are cooked by sticking in a sharp knife. They should feel almost soft.

Salade Niçoise

Serves 4

Sun-ripened vegetables makes this salad a colorful dish! Pronounced "salad nee-swahze," the recipe comes from Nice, in southern France.

YOU WILL NEED

FOR THE SALAD:

- ½ pound small potatoes
- 9 ounces green beans
- salt, black pepper
- 1 red onion
- 4 tomatoes
- 1 small green bell pepper
- 1 can tuna in natural juice (6 ounces)
- ½ head of lettuce
- 4 eggs
- 10 black olives
- small bunch of basil

FOR THE DRESSING:

- 4 tablespoons red wine vinegar
- 1 teaspoon mustard
- 1 garlic clove
- 6 tablespoons olive oil

1 Wash the potatoes, then boil them in their skins for about 15–20 minutes until they are just soft. Drain them and let them cool, then peel and slice them.

2 Wash the beans, and trim off the tops and bottoms. Cook over low heat in salted water for 10 minutes. Drain, then rinse under cold water. Now drain them again in a colander.

3 Peel and halve the onion, then slice into thin half-moons. Separate these. Wash the tomatoes, then cut pieces into eighths. Remove the stem ends. Now wash, trim, halve, and deseed the bell pepper. Cut it into strips.

4 Drain the tuna. Wash the lettuce, shake it dry, and tear it into small pieces.

5 To make the dressing, whisk the vinegar and mustard. Then crush in the garlic with a garlic press. Whisk in the olive oil a little at a time, until you have a creamy dressing.

6 Put all the vegetables into the bowl. Drizzle the dressing on top, and toss.

7 Boil four eggs for 8 minutes. When they're cold enough to touch, take off the shell, and cut each egg in half. Add to the salad.

8 FInally, add the olives and the basil, and serve.

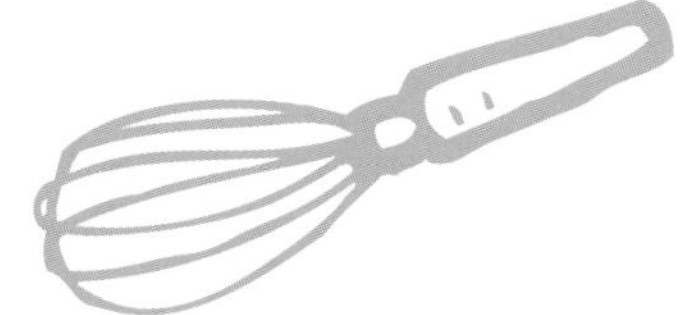

National Festivals

France has 11 national holidays a year, plus many other regional and religious festivals.

Top Holidays

National holidays honor important events in France's history. Armistice Day (November 11) marks the end of World War I. Victory Day (May 8) remembers the end of World War II. About 85 percent of French people are Roman Catholic, so religious holidays and saints' days also have festivities and traditions.

Bastille Day is celebrated with a military parade in Paris.

A dazzling fireworks display lights up the sky on Bastille Day.

Bastille Day

Bastille Day is a French national holiday and is celebrated throughout the country. It is also called Quatorze Juillet ("14th July"). Each year, the French remember July 14, 1789, when crowds stormed the Bastille prison in Paris. People were protesting against their uncaring king and queen, who had let people starve and live in poverty while they lived in luxury in grand palaces. This event sparked the French Revolution.

Like Independence Day (July 4) in the United States, Bastille Day is celebrated with firework displays, fairs, and family parties. In Paris, the French president leads a military parade, while airplanes fly in formation overhead.

DID YOU KNOW?

Since 1981, Fête de la Musique (World Music Day) has been celebrated on June 21. This is also the day when summer officially begins. In the streets, musicians play all kinds of music for free: rock, country, techno, rap, classical, and French songs.

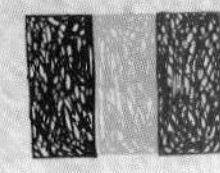

Cycle Race

Le Tour de France is the world's greatest cycle race. It starts toward the end of June each year and lasts three weeks. Cyclists from around the world compete for the "Yellow Jersey," which is given to the winner. The race covers more than 2,200 miles (3,450 kilometers) across flat, hilly, and mountainous areas in France. It sometimes visits nearby countries, too. Around 15 million people take time off work and school to gather at the roadside and cheer as the cyclists power past.

This peloton, or group of cyclists, rides the road to Col de Peyresourde in the majestic Pyrenees Mountains during Le Tour de France.

City Light Festival

The Lyon Festival of Lights is a four-day event that starts on December 8. It was first celebrated in 1852. People of Lyon set up a statue of the Virgin Mary on a hilltop and were saved from a terrible storm. Today, brightly colored light shows turn the city's famous buildings into a spectacular display.

A brilliant display of lights and images is projected onto the wall of Lyons Cathedral as part of The Festival of Lights.

Toussaint

The French celebrate Toussaint, or All Saints' Day, on November 1. This Catholic holiday honors relatives and friends who have died, as well as saints who have no special day. After attending church services, people place chrysanthemums on the graves of loved ones. Children carve jack-o'-lanterns with scary faces and trick or treat, just as they do in the United States on Halloween.

A jack-o'-lantern and cupcakes decorated with witches' hats and ghouls are part of a Toussaint celebration.

méchoui

Serves 4–6

This dish (say "may-shwee") is originally from North Africa. At village celebrations, a whole lamb is roasted on a spit, but this is a family-size version.

YOU WILL NEED

- a handful of mint
- 4 garlic cloves, plus extras
- 2 tablespoons paprika
- 3 teaspoons ground cumin
- 4 tablespoons sunflower oil or butter
- 1 small leg of lamb (about 5–6 pounds)
- salt and ground cumin for sprinkling
- rosemary sprigs, to garnish

1 First, wash the mint stalks, and shake them dry. Pull off the leaves, and chop them very finely. Peel the garlic, and put through a garlic press.

2 In a large bowl, stir the mint, garlic, paprika, cumin, and oil to make a paste.

3 Place the meat in the bowl, and rub the paste all over it. Then put the meat in a roasting dish and cover with a clean kitchen cloth. Leave it to marinate for at least 1 hour.

4 Preheat the oven to 380°F. Add a few cloves of garlic around the roast. Then cook the lamb in the oven for about 2–2½ hours, depending on its size.

5 The meat should be tender enough to pull off the bone. (Don't touch the meat until it has cooled a little.) Sprinkle the roast with salt and cumin. Garnish with rosemary, and serve.

DID YOU KNOW?

Méchoui means "barbecued lamb." In North Africa, the lamb is traditionally cooked over a fire hole or pit in the ground.

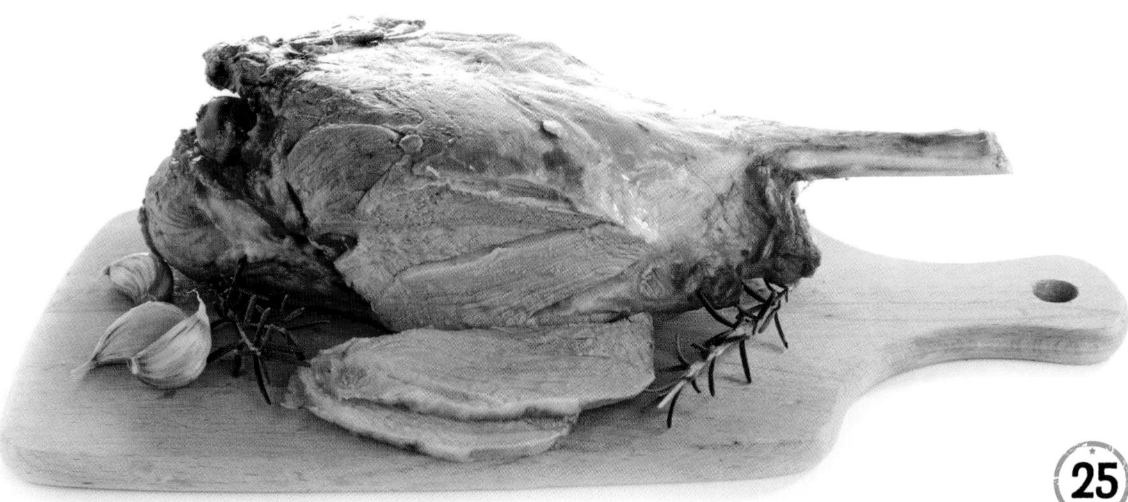

Crêpes Suzette

Makes 8 Crêpes

Crêpes are a specialty of Brittany and northern France. They are sold with different fillings at almost all fairgrounds.

YOU WILL NEED

FOR THE CRÊPES:

- 2 eggs
- 1 cup milk
- 3/4 cup all-purpose flour
- 1 tablespoon sugar
- 2 tablespoons unsalted butter

FOR THE SAUCE:

- 3 large organic oranges
- 1 cup sugar
- 2½ tablespoons unsalted butter for baking

1 Put the eggs, milk, flour, and sugar in a bowl. Stir for 3 minutes to make a thin batter. Melt the butter in a small skillet until it is golden brown, and stir it into the mixture. Set the batter aside.

2 Scrub the oranges under hot water, then pat them dry. Use a potato peeler to pare off the zest of one orange in thin strips. Squeeze out the juice. Simmer the zest, juice, and sugar in a saucepan over high heat to make a thin syrup.

DID YOU KNOW?

A crêpe is a pancake that is much thinner than an American pancake. Sweet crêpes can be filled with apples, berries, or preserves. Savory crêpes may have ham, cheese, or mushroom fillings.

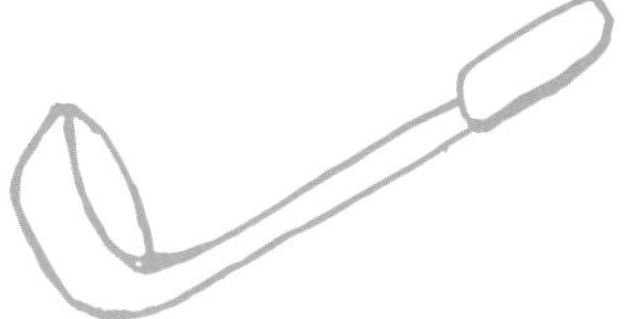

3 Peel the other two oranges, completely removing the white piths (inner skins). With a sharp knife, cut out the orange slices between their thin skins. Catch the juice.

4 Melt some of the butter in a nonstick skillet until it foams. Pour in 1 ladleful of batter. Turn the skillet, so that the batter covers the whole base. Fry the crêpe for 1 minute. Turn it over with a wooden spatula, and fry the other side for about 30 seconds.

5 Put the finished crêpe on a rack or a large plate, and cover it with a clean cloth. Fry seven more crêpes.

6 Put a few orange slices on each crêpe, and fold the crêpe over to form a small triangle. Put the crêpes back into the skillet, one at a time, and pour a little of the syrup over the top. Heat for 1 minute, and serve.

Celebrating at Home

French people love to celebrate! They prepare delicious feasts for special days, such as Christmas, New Year's Day, a wedding, or a birthday.

Slow Food

The French believe in taking their time to savor food over talk with family and friends. Traditionally, lunch and dinner have been opportunities for families to gather for a long and leisurely two-hour meal. Today, this is not always possible. But people keep the tradition whenever they can. Meal courses include: hors d'oeuvres; a soup course; cold meats called *charcuterie*; a fish dish; then a roast meat or stew. And unlike in the United States, vegetables and salad are served after the main dish! Cheeses round off the feast, followed by a dessert, such as tarte tatin.

The French often invite a family of friends over for dinner. Meals are an important way for everyone to spend quality time together.

This is the Galeries LaFayette, a famous department store in Paris. It has installed a brightly lit upside-down Christmas tree.

Christmas

On Christmas Eve, people prepare a special late meal. Then they go to church for midnight mass, a service that celebrates the birth of Christ on Christmas Day (December 25). Traditional carols are sung in the church, which is often lit with a blaze of candles. Back at home, Père Noël ("Father Christmas," or Santa Claus) leaves gifts for the children in shoes, stockings, or next to the tree. Many French homes set up a little crèche (Nativity scene) showing the baby Jesus in a manger with Mary and Joseph. The whole family helps to make this.

DID YOU KNOW?

Jour de l'An, or New Year's Day, is another holiday celebrated with a big family meal. Traditional foods such as pancakes and foie gras (goose liver) are said to bring good luck for the new year.

Saying "I Do!"

Traditionally, people in France get married in a church or chapel. Before the ceremony, the groom meets the bride at her home, and they walk to the church. Children block their way by holding up white ribbons, which the bride must cut with scissors: This symbolizes breaking through obstacles in life. At the ceremony, the groom walks his mother down the aisle as a sign of respect. Then, at the reception, the bride and groom lean over a cake called a croquembouche ("crunch in the mouth"). This is a cone of profiteroles (cream-filled pastries). If they can kiss without knocking the cake over, they will have a long and happy life together.

This croquembouche wedding cake is decorated with threads of caramel and flowers.

Regional Fêtes

Every area of France has its own fête, or festival, that celebrates the harvest or another important event. Traditionally, people in rural areas contribute to the occasion by making food and bringing drinks for a big, communal meal.

Today, even though many people work in industries other than farming, the custom continues. Sometimes hundreds of people gather for a meal. The fête can last for days, with music, dancing, local crafts—and even more food!

Crowds of people dressed in white and red gather at the five-day summer festival of Bayonne (Fêtes de Bayonne).

Mother's Day

The French tradition of Mother's Day is said to have started in 1806, when emperor Napoleon Bonaparte announced a special day for children to honor their mothers. Today, people give their mothers chocolates, flowers, cakes, and original poems. They may also treat their mom to a special meal, whether home-cooked or at a nice restaurant.

People give each other sprays of lily of the valley on May 1. In the language of flowers, lily of the valley means "return of happiness."

Duck Breast

Serves 4

This classic dish from southwestern France is a favorite meal to serve on special occasions, such as birthdays. It's easy to cook and delicious!

YOU WILL NEED

- 3 tablespoons lemon juice
- 2 tablespoons runny honey
- salt, black pepper
- 2 duck breast fillets (about 10 ounces each)
- 2 tablespoons cooking oil
- a handful of shallots, diced
- scallion slices, to garnish

TOP TIP

You can also cook duck in an oven preheated to 400°F. Prick the skin with a fork. Place on a rack, skin side down, and put a baking dish underneath to catch drippings. Roast for 20–30 minutes.

1 Put the lemon juice, honey, salt, and pepper in a bowl, and stir. Wash the duck breasts under cold water, and pat them dry. Put them in a large ovenproof dish then rub all over with the marinade. Cover the dish with plastic wrap, and chill in the refrigerator for 2 hours.

2 Remove the fillets from the marinade, and pat them dry. Set the marinade aside. Preheat the oven to 200°F.

3 Heat the oil over medium heat in a skillet. Put the fillets in, skin side down, and fry them for about 7 minutes. Turn them over and fry for another 5–7 minutes.

4 Place the duck breasts on a serving platter and cover. Put them in the preheated oven.

5 Peel and slice the shallots. Fry them in the skillet over medium heat until they look see-through. Add 5 tablespoons water. Using a wooden spoon, loosen the meat juices in the skillet. Add the marinade, and bring the sauce to a boil. Season with salt and pepper.

6 Cut the duck breast into slices. Set on a platter, and pour some sauce on top. Scatter the scallion slices around.

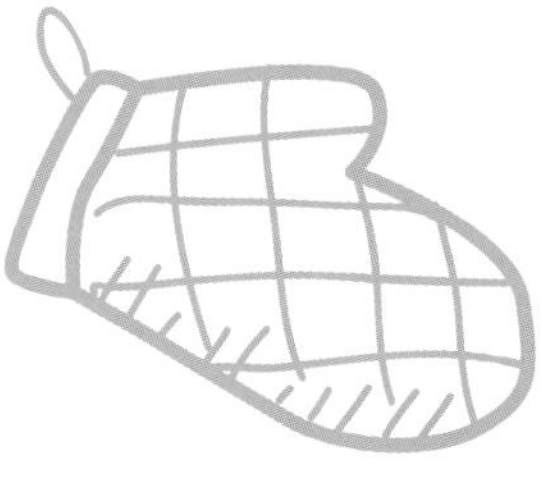

Chocolate Mousse

Serves 4–6

Make this delicious dessert for a party or birthday. Its creamy smoothness makes a delectable chocolate treat!

YOU WILL NEED

- 5 ounces milk chocolate or semisweet chocolate (or half of each)
- 2 large eggs
- 2 tablespoons confectioner's sugar
- 1/2 cup whipping cream or heavy cream
- 1 teaspoon vanilla extract
- whipped cream and cocoa powder, to serve

1 Chop the chocolate into medium-size pieces, then put them into a small bowl.

2 Put some water into a saucepan that is slightly larger than the bowl, and bring it to a boil.

3 Put the bowl in the saucepan, and stir the chocolate continuously as it melts. Take the pan off the heat.

4 Separate the eggs. Using a whisk, beat the egg whites until they are stiff. Slowly sprinkle in the sugar while you whisk, then chill the egg whites in the refrigerator. Now whisk the cream until stiff, and chill it in the refrigerator.

5 In a large bowl, whisk the egg yolks and the vanilla extract until they are creamy. Add in the melted chocolate, stirring continuously.

TOP TIP

You can choose any chocolate you like. Try making the mousse with white chocolate or chocolate flavored with orange or mint.

6 Put the stiff cream on top of the chocolate mixture. Gently stir it in with a whisk or spoon.

7 Now put the stiff egg whites on top. Very gently, stir them into the mixture with a spoon. Don't mix or whisk, or the mousse will collapse.

8 Chill the mousse in the refrigerator for at least 3 hours. Spoon it into glasses, and serve.

Daily Life in France

French people live in cities, towns, and villages or on farms and vineyards. They work hard and study hard at school. In their free time, they enjoy sports, games—and summer vacations!

Paris Power

Life in big cities such as Paris, Lyon, and Marseilles can be crowded and busy. In Paris, the capital of France, people commute (travel) into town from the surrounding suburbs. Many ride the bus or the Métro, a train system with 303 stations. Stores, galleries, and office buildings line the wide boulevards of Paris. People eat at cafés and restaurants, which serve French and world cuisines. They also buy delicious fresh bread at *boulangeries*, or bakeries.

Paris is a bustling capital city known for its cafés, shops, museums, and historical sites. Its buildings have unique architectural designs.

Many families get away from the cities in August and go camping in the countryside.

Getting Away

The French treasure their vacation time, when they can take a break from daily life and relax with the family. Most people have five weeks vacation from work a year. Traditionally, the French take off the whole month of August and head for a beautiful spot.

The coastal towns along the French Riviera are popular destinations. Other favorite places are lake resorts and the mountains. Some people have their own summer homes in the country, and some stay with friends. Camping out under the stars is popular, too, since France can get up to 100°F (38°C) in August. People may also vacation in nearby countries, such as Italy, Austria, Switzerland, Spain, or the United Kingdom.

DID YOU KNOW?

Paris is the most densely populated city in Europe. Plus, around 30 million tourists roam through its streets sightseeing each year!

People have fun swimming and sunbathing on the beach of Annecy Lake. It is one of the most popular resorts in France.

Big Sports

Football (called "soccer" in the United States) is a huge sport in France. People avidly follow their local and national teams, and a game between rival teams is a huge event. Rugby is another favorite team sport. The French are also good at sailing, fencing, car racing, and tennis.

People take advantage of France's varied landscape by swimming in lakes and rivers, and sailing along the coast. They also go fishing, hiking, rock climbing, and caving inland. Skiing and mountain climbing are popular in the Alps and Pyrenees Mountains.

Pétanque is a game that started in Provence. It uses colored balls and is similar to boules, or lawn bowling.

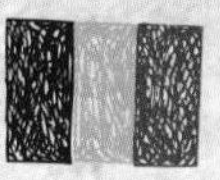

French schoolchildren visit the Louvre Museum in Paris. It has some of the most famous statues and paintings in the world.

School Days

Learning starts early in France. In many families, both parents work, so babies and toddlers go to day-care centers during the week. Young children go to *maternelle*, or preschool. This is a good chance for them to interact with other children and learn social skills. At six years old, elementary school starts, where writing, math, history, and geography are learned. From 11 to 14 years old, children go to *collège*, where languages and IT are studied, too. Next comes the *lycée*, where students take *le bac*, a difficult exam. When they pass, it's like graduating from high school.

But it's not all hard work. Schoolchildren often go on class trips to visit museums and historic places. At palaces like Versailles, they learn about how kings and queens lived and ruled France.

DID YOU KNOW?

French is a main language in many countries: Benin, Burkina Faso, Central African Republic, both Congos, Côte d'Ivoire, Gabon, Guinea, Luxembourg, Mali, Monaco, Niger, Senegal, and Togo. It is also spoken in Quebec, Canada.

Onion Soup

Serves 6

This is an everyday soup—but oh-so yummy! The French often grow onions in their yard, which give this soup a super-fresh flavor.

YOU WILL NEED

- 2 large white onions
- 2 tablespoons duck or goose fat
- 4 ounces Cantal cheese or Monterey Jack cheese
- 4 ounces Gruyère cheese
- French bread, a day or two old and a little stale
- salt, pepper

1 Peel and chop the onions. Put the duck fat into a large saucepan, and heat it over medium heat. Now add the onions. Fry them over low heat until they are a golden color. Keep stirring as you fry.

2 Put about 2–2½ quarts water in the saucepan. Season the soup with salt and pepper. Cover the saucepan with a lid, and simmer the soup over low heat for 25 minutes.

TOP TIP

This soup is usually made with Cantal, from the French Auvergne region. It has a strong, earthy flavor. Gruyère is tangy and great for melting.

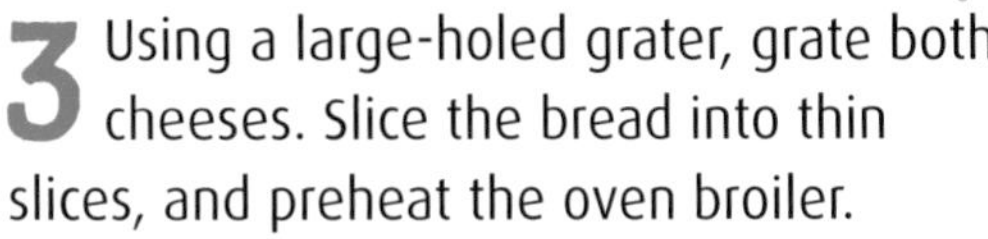

3 Using a large-holed grater, grate both cheeses. Slice the bread into thin slices, and preheat the oven broiler.

4 Put a layer of bread and a layer of cheese into ovenproof soup bowls. Repeat until you've used up all the cheese. Pour the soup on top.

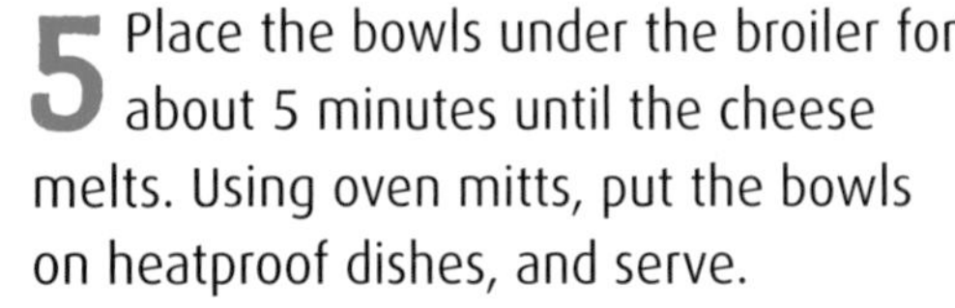

5 Place the bowls under the broiler for about 5 minutes until the cheese melts. Using oven mitts, put the bowls on heatproof dishes, and serve.

40-Clove Chicken

Serves 4

You may be surprised that this dish uses 40 cloves of garlic! But the sharp tang of fresh garlic mellows as it cooks, leaving an earthy taste.

YOU WILL NEED

- 1 large chicken (about 3½ pounds)
- salt, black pepper
- ½ bunch parsley
- few sprigs of thyme
- 40 garlic cloves (3–4 heads)
- 2 bay leaves
- ½ organic lemon
- 4 tablespoons olive oil
- 1–2 cups chicken broth
- ½ bunch dill, to garnish

1 Preheat the oven to 450°F. Season the chicken inside and out with salt and pepper. Rinse the parsley and thyme, and tear the leaves off the stalks. Peel and roughly chop four of the garlic cloves.

2 Push the chopped garlic, parsley, thyme, bay leaves, and the half lemon into the chicken cavity.

3 Pour the oil into a large Dutch oven. Place the chicken into the dish, and turn it in the oil to coat it all over. Place the chicken breast side down.

4 Wash the remaining garlic heads with their skin on. Then cut each head in half (or separate out the cloves), and place them next to the chicken. Roast the chicken and garlic for 30 minutes.

5 Turn the chicken over, and pour the broth into the dish. Roast for another 30–40 minutes or until the chicken is completely cooked.

6 Check to see if the chicken is cooked. Prick the fattest part of a leg with a skewer, and pull it out. If the juices are pink, the chicken needs more cooking. If they are clear, it is done. Garnish with the dill, and serve with the roasted garlic.

SAFETY TIP

Always wash your hands with soap and warm water after handling raw chicken. Wash all cutting boards and utensils used to prepare raw chicken, too.

Tarte Tatin

Makes 1 tart

This upside-down apple tart is totally tasty! It is delicious served hot, straight from the oven. But it is also excellent served cold. Try it with ice cream.

YOU WILL NEED

- 2/3 cup chilled butter
- 1 1/8 cups all-purpose flour (plus more for the work surface)
- 1 pinch baking powder
- 2 tablespoons sugar
- 1 pinch salt
- 1 egg yolk
- 2 1/4 pounds Golden Delicious apples
- 1 1/8 cups confectioner's sugar

PLUS:

- ovenproof pie plate, 11 inches (28 cm) in diameter

1 Cut ¼ cup butter into cubes. Mix the butter, flour, baking powder, sugar, salt, and egg yolk to make a smooth dough. Shape into a ball. Cover in plastic wrap, and chill for 1 hour.

2 Preheat the oven to 450°F. Peel and quarter the apples, cutting out the cores. Sprinkle the base of the pie plate with confectioner's sugar. Bake in the center of the oven for 10 minutes, until the sugar turns a golden caramel color. Put the rest of the butter in the plate, and let it melt.

DID YOU KNOW?

This tart was invented by mistake by the Tatin sisters, who worked in a hotel in France. They were very busy and forgot to put the dough into the plate first when they were making an apple tart.

3 Lay out the apple pieces, with the rounded side down, on top of the caramel. Bake for about 5 minutes in the center of the oven.

4 Next, lightly flour your work surface, and roll out the dough. Make a circle a little larger than the pie plate. Take the pie plate out of the oven, and turn the heat down to 400°F.

5 Using a rolling pin to help, lift the dough onto the apples. Press down lightly around the edge, and prick the top several times with a fork. Bake the tart for about 30 minutes.

6 Ask your assistant to help with this step. First, take the tart out of the oven. Put a large round platter on top, then quickly turn over both pie plate and platter, holding them together tightly. Remove the plate, and serve.

Glossary

Armistice Day (November 11) A national holiday that celebrates the end of World War I in 1918.

Bastille Day (July 14) A national holiday that celebrates the storming of the Bastille prison in Paris on July 14, 1789. It sparked the French Revolution.

boulangerie A bakery that sells fresh bread.

charcuterie Cold cooked meats made from pork and other animal meats.

crêpe suzette A sweet pancake from northern France and Brittany.

croquembouche A French wedding cake that is a tall pyramid stacked with cream-filled pastries. It is decorated with caramel threads and fresh flowers.

French Revolution (1789–1799) A civil war that brought about major changes in the French government. People rebelled against the king and queen.

gratin A dish made with cheese or cream. It is baked in the oven, where the cheese melts into a crust.

Le bac An exam that students take before they graduate from the French equivalent of high school.

méchoui A North African dish of whole marinated and barbecued lamb.

pétanque A popular French game played with colored metal balls.

Tarte Tatin An upside-down tart with caramelized apples that comes from central France. It is named after the Tatin sisters, who made up the recipe.

Tour de France An annual French bicycle race that lasts for three weeks. The race takes place on flat, hilly, and mountainous areas.

Toussaint (November 1) Toussaint (All Saints' Day) is celebrated by visiting the graves of family members who have died.

Victory Day (May 8) A day that celebrates France's freedom from German rule at the end of World War II in 1945.

Further Resources

Books

Colson, Mary.
France (Countries Around the World).
Heinemann, Portsmouth, NH: 2011.

Demi.
Joan of Arc.
Marshall Cavendish Children, Tarrytown, NY: 2011.

Howse, Jennifer.
Palace of Versailles: Home to the Kings of France (Castles of the World).
Av2 by Weigl, New York: 2015.

Lonely Planet.
Not For Parents Paris: Everything You Ever Wanted to Know.
Lonely Planet, Oakland, CA: 2011.

Roholt, Christine VeLure.
French Food (I Can Cook!).
Smart Apple Media, Mankato, MN: 2012.

Websites

Due to the changing nature of Internet links, PowerKids Press has developed an online list of websites related to the subject of this book. This site is updated regularly. Please use this link to access the list:

www.powerkidslinks.com/lc/france

Index